CLERICAL VESTMENTS

CEREMONIAL DRESS OF THE CHURCH

Sarah Bailey

SHIRE PUBLICATIONS

Published in Great Britain in 2013 by Shire Publications Ltd, Midland House, West Way, Botley, Oxford OX2 0PH, United Kingdom.

43-01 21st Street, Suite 220B, Long Island City, NY 11101, USA.

E-mail: shire@shirebooks.co.uk   www.shirebooks.co.uk

A CIP catalogue record for this book is available from the British Library.

Shire Library no. 727.   ISBN-13: 978 0 74781 221 0

Sarah Bailey has asserted her right under the Copyright, Designs and Patents Act, 1988, to be identified as the author of this book.

Designed by Tony Truscott Designs, Sussex, UK and typeset in Perpetua and Gill Sans.

Printed in China through Worldprint Ltd.

13 14 15 16 17   10 9 8 7 6 5 4 3 2 1

COVER IMAGE
The pelican pecks her breast which drips blood to feed her young. The pelican came to symbolise the Passion of Jesus and the Eucharist and usurped the image of the lamb and flag.

TITLE PAGE IMAGE
The superb embellishment of these bishops' vestments includes fur edging, bejewelled mitres and morses and, just visible, the elegant 'pineapple' design fabric of a tunic. Church Stretton.

CONTENTS PAGE IMAGE
Blaize, Bishop of Sebasta in Armenia, leads a procession accompanied by three colleagues wearing black Geneva gowns and preaching tabs. Bishop Blaise wears his mitre and cope. Print of 1814 by R. Havell.

ACKNOWLEDGEMENTS
I would like to thank Chrissie White and Reverend Justin Bailey for their kind assistance with research and the following for allowing me to use illustrations:

Abbortsford House, page 14 (top), 49; Reverend Angus Adamson, Brodick Church, page 28 (left); All Saints Church, Newland, Forest of Dean, page 46; Reverend Justin Bailey, pages 11 (left), 25 (top and bottom right), 36 (bottom), 60 (bottom); Marie Brisou, Aloisio Brito Photography and St Paul's Cathedral, page 41; The monks of Downside Abbey, page 15; Netta Ewing and The Sacred Threads Group, page 45, 60 (top), 61; Glasgow Museums, page 20 (bottom), 59 (top); Rozanne Hawksley, page 59 (bottom); Juliet Hemingray, page 38; Richard Luzar at Luzar Vestments, page 14 (bottom), 25 (left); Judith Peacock, page 42; Victoria and Albert Museum, pages 17, 32, 50; The Walters Art Museum, Maryland, page 24; Reverend Ron Wood for his cartoons, pages 6 (top) and 63. All other images are from the author's collection.

CONTENTS

TEXTILES AND THE CHURCH

FROM THE simple altar linen in a rural church to the gloriously elaborate copes worn on festal occasions in cathedrals throughout Europe, textiles in one form or another have been used in Christian worship for centuries. These ecclesiastical textiles fall into two main categories: the paraments, that is, the altar frontals, pulpit and lectern fall and banners; and the vestments, the garments worn by the clergy and lay officiants during a church service. Although at times throughout their development these vestments may have appeared primarily to reflect the status and wealth of the clergy, these garments were made for the service of God, service by his servants.

Clerical vestments inform a congregation about the leader of their worship. The chasuble or cope can help to focus attention, for example, on a particular gesture, for example a symbolic action during the Eucharist, or may subtly add to the mood of a specific festival or service. They serve a useful purpose in identifying the officiant whilst lessening their individuality – the priest being a representative of the people. The role of the priest, of whichever denomination, is that of an intercessor, one who prays on behalf of the congregation. Some vestments, especially copes, can lend grandeur and solemnity to the proceedings, enhancing the experience of worship and adding to the mystery of the divine service whilst their colours hint at the seasonal changes of the church year. On the other hand the cassock and specifically the 'dog collar' are the day-to-day uniform of the clergy and are very recognisable as such, defining the wearer's role and marking him or her out from the crowd.

The Roman Catholic church, the Eastern Orthodox church and the various denominations of the Anglican Church, including the Church of England, all have their own traditions as far as vestments are concerned. All Christians were part of the Church in Rome until the Protestant Reformation, a sixteenth-century schism within Western Christianity initiated by Martin Luther, John Calvin and other early Protestants which led to the creation of new national Protestant churches, and the plethora of churches that exists in the twenty-first century.

Opposite: Bourges Cathedral has some of the most beautiful stained-glass windows in Western Europe, which are invaluable for the study of contemporary costume. The bishop here wears a conical mitre, a chasuble and an omophorion.

'And what do you do?' asked the VIP. For those who regularly attend churches that use them, vestments may still be seen. However, some people are rather bemused by the exotic garments.

In Western Europe some early ecclesiastical textiles still exist, mainly in public museums and cathedral treasuries but also in small parish churches, cared for and preserved for education and study as well as use. Much of the information on early priestly clothing is gleaned from brasses, sculptures, stained glass and paintings of the Middle Ages giving clues to how clerical vestments developed. Although there are regional variations, the development of vestments follows a fairly straightforward path. The Church can take centuries to adopt new ideas

and once something has become tradition it is often there to stay, but as new fabrics became available so fashions in clerical garments have changed too.

The following chapters provide a brief overview of clothing worn by the clergy since the beginning of their use in the Christian faith mainly but not exclusively in Britain, looking at fabrics, embellishment and some of the individuals who make these vestments.

Left: Anglican choir dress typically consists of the cassock, surplice, tippet or scarf and academic hood.

Below: There are huge variations in vestments – catholic, orthodox or protestant. This print from the 1870s gives some idea of the differences between denominations over time and across Europe.

THE EVOLUTION OF CLERICAL VESTMENTS

IN THE FOURTH CENTURY AD St Jerome wrote about what a priest should wear in the temple:

> We ought not to go into the sanctuary just as we please, and in our ordinary clothes, defiled with the visage of common life, but with clear conscience and clean garments handle the sacraments of the Lord.

Vestments can be split into a few distinct groups: those used specifically at the Eucharist and for other sacraments; the garments used for non-sacramental occasions; the clothes which denote specific rank or role; and lastly the garments which form customary clerical costume, clothing used on non-liturgical occasions. There is something mysterious and magical about a service where many clergy are robed in their finery and gathered together for worship. Many of the worship garments are part of a church's history and frequently predate the vicar by a couple of centuries. Because of the costly nature of production (both historically and now) vestments are often now over-mended and patched up but always cared for and carefully kept. Due to this care, Britain especially has a rich heritage of this type of costume which is viewed and used, not kept in pristine museum conditions, but touched and valued.

Fashion and available material, plus the usefulness – or use – of some garments affects what has survived. All vestments were originally derived from everyday clothing. Styles of clothing change over time, and as clergy continued to wear an item that was no longer in general use, it then became traditional, and symbolic rather than utilitarian. Looking at clerical vesture is akin to looking at living history in that the garments, though now perhaps highly stylised and ornamented, have not essentially changed in centuries. Progression can easily be seen and understood.

Most items of vesture can be traced back to the Roman Empire and the ordinary dress of a Roman citizen. Development from lay attire to that used by the priesthood took place between the fourth and ninth centuries AD.

Opposite:
The external stone carving on Chartres Cathedral shows clergy wearing chasubles and embroidered apparels, stoles and mitres. The stone carving is so precise that the embroidered decoration is very easy to see.

Canonicus Regularis Ordinis S. GILBERTI.
755.

Although this is an eighteenth-century print it shows the earlier dress of a canon wearing a fur-edged cloak. The modern black clerical cloak is still a heavy wool garment usually used for any outside duties such as burial.

As well as this natural development, changes made to the religious rites themselves as well as the ceremonial would have necessitated changes in vestments too. Generally the vestments used today are relatively little changed from the garments originally established as those worn by the clergy. Fabrics, surface embellishment and shapes may have fluctuated but what the congregation of an English cathedral sees now has changed little over centuries. It would be difficult to follow the development of liturgical dress were it not for depictions of dress in frescoes, bronze and marble, as there are not many surviving examples of textiles from the very early period. The surviving examples from earliest times are those that have been hidden and protected – from destruction or secular reuse – over the centuries by monasteries or individuals.

During the Reformation a few went further than many people thought really necessary, meaning that vestments suffered the fate of many pieces of ecclesiastical art. It is recorded that Grindal, archbishop at York (1570) and then archbishop of Canterbury (1575), ensured the destruction of 'vestments, albs, tunicles, stoles, phanons and every kind of Eucharistic accessory.' The impact of the Reformation in Britain cannot be underestimated and although this meant a period in which the more elaborate vestments almost vanished from view, they did not disappear entirely. Some were hidden away for a time until it became safe to use them once more and others continued to be used in places away from the zeal of the reformers. In Western Europe today there is a vast range of worship styles and a mix of vestment usage. In Britain especially, there is a resurgent interest in the design of vestments.

ALB

The *Tunica alba* began life as traditional Roman garb, literally a 'white tunic' with long sleeves worn by men of upper classes in the second and third centuries, the length of the sleeves ensuring that manual labour would be difficult. The fabric was gathered into a narrow neckband with a front opening which fastened with a fibula or pin or loops and buttons. It was usually cut in one piece rather than having separate sleeves. Linen and wool were the usual fabrics but in AD 265 it was recorded that the Emperor Gallienus (AD 260–8) made a gift to his eventual successor Claudius (AD 268–70) of a tunic of silk woven with wool or cotton (the fabric being known as *sub-serica*). Herbert Norris

Eagerly, yet fearfully, his lips approach the nectar divine.

in his book *Church Vestments: their Origin and Development* notes that the use of the word alb came into common practice in association with ecclesiastical use in a canon of the Council of Carthage (*c.* 400). This is possibly one of the earliest rules regarding vestments in ritual use. The alb is worn with a cincture around the waist. In the eleventh and twelfth centuries the attachment of apparels to the alb became increasingly common. Apparels were decorative bands at the hem and wrist, often highly embroidered or woven. Examples can frequently be seen on early statuary, effigies and stained glass. Referring to the range of coloured albs being used, Winchelsey, archbishop of Canterbury (1294–1313), had albs of the liturgical colours, corresponding with other vestments. This has gone out of use in modern times so we rarely see coloured albs used in church today.

Above left: A priest wears a plain white hooded alb with the green stole of Ordinary Time or Trinity for a pet service.

Above: A jolly monk wearing a plain alb with cincture, from which hangs his rosary, and the scapular typical of many monastic orders.

AMICE

This is a rectangle of linen fabric with ties at either end which is wrapped around the neck like a scarf. The amice may still be worn if the alb does not cover a priest's everyday clothing. Besides the surplice, it was one of the first items to be adorned with embroidered or woven bands of decoration and was called the 'apparelled amice'. The decorated section stood up like a stiff collar and although the apparelled amice is no longer widely used it can be

Memorial brasses are an excellent source of information on the vestments of the Middle Ages. The apparelled amice, alb and chasuble are very ornate here and had not changed in their style for several centuries up to the creation of this monument, which is in Sutton Coldfield church and was created for the bishop of Exeter who died in 1554.

seen in many church sculptures and stained-glass windows. These sculptures give a good idea of the embroidered amices and surplices which were worn by priests underneath the chasuble and stole.

CASSOCK OR SOUTANE

This is often the garment worn by priests on a day-to-day basis for funerals, the offices and in public. This item of clerical clothing is worn by priests of the Roman Catholic Church, Eastern Orthodox Church, Anglican Church and Lutheran Church, and some ministers and ordained officers of Presbyterian and Reformed churches. Made of a thick black fabric and ankle-length, it often has thirty-three buttons down the front to represent the length of Christ's life in years. The word 'cassock' comes from Middle French 'casaque', meaning a long coat. In Ireland and in several other English-speaking countries, it is also known by the French-derived word 'soutane'. A sash, known also as a fascia, may be worn with the cassock. In 1850, the year in

Roman Catholic bishops in 1922 wearing soutane or cassock, pelligrina or shoulder cape and the biretta – the hat with central pompom. Three also wear a tasselled fascia, the wide belt – many earlier images of the fascia show them decorated with tiny bells.

which he restored the Catholic hierarchy in England and Wales, Pope Pius IX was understood to grant to all priests in England and Wales the privilege of wearing a replica of his white caped cassock, in black. Since then, the wearing of the pellegrina shoulder cape with the cassock has been the sign of a Catholic priest in England, Wales, Scotland, Ireland, Australia, and New Zealand. In Anglican churches, a black cassock is the norm, but other colours and variations are common.

CHASUBLE

The chasuble developed from the *paenula* (later called the *casula* or 'little house' from which comes its modern name), a circular garment reaching the hands, with a central hole for the head. Looking at the shape of the chasuble one can almost imagine its evolution. Like a highly decorative poncho, it is one of the garments most visible during a church service. The primitive chasuble was bell-shaped or conical with the seam concealed beneath an orphrey, an embroidered or woven band. A set of Mass vestments always includes a chasuble and matching stole, the decoration of each reflecting the other, although during the Middle Ages the stole and maniple (see page 21) were of contrasting colour to the chasuble.

There are many fine examples of early chasubles in sculptures in churches and cathedrals all across Europe, showing the elaborate decoration and embroidery not only on the chasubles themselves but also on the stoles which are part of the 'set'. These examples also give an insight into the shape of the chasubles and copes that were favoured at particular times.

Chasubles and copes – being the richest and most decorative garments worn by priests – are made of damasks, brocades or cut velvets which fall into graceful folds, and are lined with silks – in the case of the chasuble often in a contrasting colour. If the chasuble fabric needed more body it was – and still is – usual to use a linen fabric as an interlining.

The *Inventory of Henry Fitzroy, Duke of Richmond and Somerset* (*c.* 1550) provides a glimpse of the splendour of vestments provided for Henry's private chapel. Among the *'Chapelle Stuff'* are the following items – the vestment referred to most probably being a chasuble. This reference gives some idea of the magnificence and importance of a small

There are amazing details regarding clerical dress in many early sculptures. This twelfth-century carved stone section shows St Hilary, the founding bishop of Poitiers, wearing his decorated chasuble with a maniple over his right arm.

These chasubles belonged to Cardinal Newman (1801–90) and are now kept at Abbotsford House, Scotland (see also page 49). They are of an earlier period with some very fine embroidery.

Green gothic Low Mass chasuble with machine-embroidered panels of chalice and host in gold tones with rather elaborate decorative embroidery.

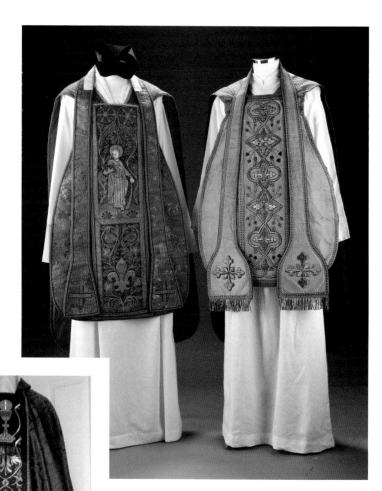

number of vestments. Items like these were included in treasuries of great houses (with chapels) as well as larger churches and cathedrals and due to their costliness were listed as separate items alongside silverware, tapestries and other prized possessions:

> Item, a Vestyment of cloth of golde of Damask and crymsen velwet pirled, with all thinges thereunto apperteynyng.

> Item, ij. Chesipples for the deacon and subdeacon, of the same stuff, with all thinges to them belonging.

Item, a Vestyment of purple velvet, with angelles and floures, with all thinges to the same belonging.

Item, ij. Chesipples for the deacon and subdeacon, belonging to the same vestiment.

The first development in the shape of the chasuble came when the sides were shortened to allow for easier movement of the hands and arms. This became the Gothic shape, with front and back coming almost to a point and reaching to the ankles. This shape persisted for many years but then, as more fabric was removed to allow for more unrestricted movement, by the eighteenth century, and principally on the continent, a shape known as fiddleback was adopted. The fiddleback chasuble has a roughly rectangular shape at the back and a 'fiddleback' shape at the front to allow for much easier movement of the arms. The adoption of this new shape allowed the use of much stiffer and heavily embellished fabrics. This persisted until the mid-Victorian resurgence of everything Gothic and the reestablishment of a more

A heavily embroidered orphrey adorns this chasuble in an altar panel by Hans Memling (1491). Clearly shown are the richly bejewelled mitre and, on his left arm, a fairly long maniple.

Detail of an orphrey made by the Sisters of the Poor Child Jesus at Southam, near Rugby in Warwickshire, in 1895, and showing exquisite embroidery skill. Downside Abbey.

The chasuble as
it developed from
its Roman origins
(a) through the
conical type (b);
the shortening
of the sides (c);
the exaggerated
fiddleback shape
(d/e); and finally
re-embracing the
modern Gothic
shape (f).

A red Gothic
chasuble of the
early twentieth
century made from
a plain brocade,
with Y-shaped
orphreys
of gold fabric
outlined with
a very common
'dice' braid.

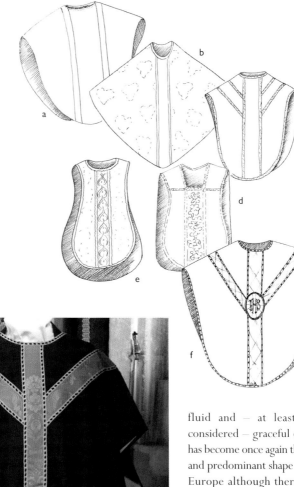

fluid and – at least generally
considered – graceful design. This
has become once again the preferred
and predominant shape for western
Europe although there are many
Roman or fiddleback chasubles
still in use. One alternative to the
chasuble that has appeared over the
last thirty years is the development
of a single wide orphrey hanging
front and back over a plain chasuble.
This falls from a wide band sitting
on the shoulders and is similar to a
monastic scapular, essentially two
rectangles of fabric caught together
at the shoulders.

COPE

Although one of the most splendid garments seen in church surroundings, the cope is in essence a simple garment. The early medieval version was a cape used by priests in bad weather. It is a semi-circle of fabric, initially with a usable hood which, by the fifteenth century, became a flat flap of fabric attached to the back of the cope with buttons. This false hood and the orphreys which are attached to the front edges generally have the richest decoration. A cope may use a damask or brocade with embroidered orphreys and hood, traditionally worked onto linen fabric in silks and metal threads. We have almost come full circle since the apex of Opus Anglicanum (fine needlework of Medieval England often using gold and silver threads on rich velvet or linen grounds, see 'Embroidered Decoration') and the fantastically embroidered copes of the thirteenth and fourteenth centuries, and there are now examples of very fine modern copes, painted, printed and embroidered. Conrad, abbot of Canterbury, gave a cope to that cathedral in 1108 that was 'embroidered with gold, and having a fringe of one hundred and forty silver bells'. Exeter Cathedral had seventy-four copes in regular use in 1327. Extant examples in museums around the world show that the shape has changed little; it started life as a conical, bell-shaped garment which became a more fluid and softer shape as the heavily embroidered vestment went out and woven fabrics became more prevalent. Today much lighter fabrics are used, which can be printed, woven or embroidered.

Butler Bowden Cope (c. 1330–50), depicting scenes from the life of the Virgin and richly embroidered with pearls, glass and metal threads. Victoria and Albert Museum.

This 1882 image shows the semi-circular pattern of the cope and a variety of caps.

Mention must be made of the *Morse*, a cope fastening, usually listed as a separate item in cathedral treasuries throughout Europe. Early examples from Limoges from the thirteenth and fourteenth centuries are richly ornamented fastenings in gold and enamels of the most exquisite craftsmanship.

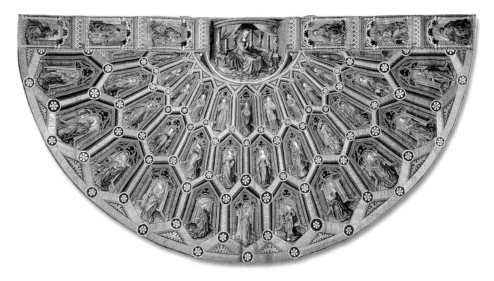

Above: The Cope of Saint John from the vestments of the Order of the Golden Fleece. Created between 1433 and 1442, probably in the workshop of Thierry du Chastel and designed by Robert Campin. It has gold, silver and silk embroidery, pearls, glass beads and velvet applique onto linen and is now in the Kunsthistorisches Museum, Vienna.

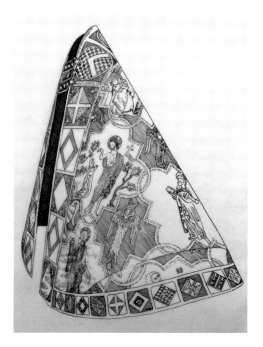

Left: The Syon Cope is a bell-shaped cope of the early fourteenth century. It has a linen base and is embroidered with silk, silver gilt and silver threads.

Below: A French fifteenth-century morse – a clasp for a cope, often enamelled and jewelled.

DALMATIC (AND TUNICLE)

The tabard-like dalmatic first appeared in the third century AD, taking its form from contemporary secular garments. Both the dalmatic and the tunicle became standard wear for the deacon and subdeacon assisting the priest in all Christian churches soon after their appearance. According to Walafrid Strabo, writing in the ninth century, priests wore dalmatics before chasubles became the vestment of choice. Gradually it became

Above: The tunicle and dalmatic are basically the same garment, the dalmatic sometimes having extra bands of decoration.

Right: Embroidered orphreys depicting the life of the Virgin Mary. The dalmatic is from a set of vestments from Whalley Abbey, Lancashire, England, a Cistercian monastery founded in 1296. Glasgow Museums collection.

accepted that whilst priests wore the chasuble their deacons and
subdeacons wore the dalmatic (and tunicle) to assist during Mass.

Decoration of various types has ornamented the dalmatic but one thing
which has remained is the use of two vertical bands front and back, which
were originally red in colour. In the Middle Ages fabrics and decoration
became far more elaborate than the original linen, wool or cotton, the
dalmatics being made of gold cloth with perhaps tasselled decoration. In
modern usage, the dalmatic may be seen being worn by a bishop and deacon
over an alb, and the tunicle by the subdeacon, acolytes and minor clerics.
These garments are still seen today as part of a Mass set.

This mass set includes a Baroque-style chasuble flanked by a dalmatic and tunicle. Museo del Carmen de Maipú, Santiago de Chile. Photo: Jorge Barrios.

MANIPLE

This item started life as a cloth used by the priest to wipe the face and
hands during a service. It appears to have been used in the Roman liturgy
since at least the sixth century and soon developed into a smaller version
of the stole with equivalent surface decoration, which included a cross. It
was worn over the arm as can be seen on many stone carvings in cathedrals
throughout Europe. It has largely fallen out of use today, in most places
having become an encumbrance rather than an enhancement to worship.
Some of the most ornate versions are those made in France and Italy in

the nineteenth century and have incredibly weighty, three-dimensional embroidery frequently with bullion (a heavy metal fringing most commonly used in the twenty-first century for military uniforms) and galloons (a decorative woven trim made of metallic gold or silver thread, lace, or embroidery). The maniple was made optional in the Roman Catholic Church in 1967.

The elaborate
detail in this print
shows the layers
worn by the
bishop, with his
maniple, gloves
and a triangular
embroidered
mitre.

MITRE

The mitre is reserved for bishops and mitred abbots. It started life as an odd mixture of crown and hat and is said to have originated from the Jewish *mitznet*. The first triangular mitre appears in the thirteenth century and gradually evolved into its now-familiar shape. Herbert Norris in his book, *Church Vestments*, refers to the exorbitant amounts paid for mitres by some clergy. 'John Peckham, Archbishop of Canterbury – and he a Franciscan! – paid £173 4s 1d. for a mitre in 1288,' which must have been of exceptional magnificence. After the Reformation the mitre fell out of favour within the Protestant church; it was re-introduced into Anglican churches with the Oxford Movement in the late nineteenth century, however, and continues

Far left: Tradition was for a decorative band to be run around the crown of the head. This band was called the *circulus*. Another band extended at right angles to the circulus, forming an upside-down 'T'. This vertical ornamentation was called the *titulus*. Often, the *circulus* and *titulus* were lavishly embroidered. Tours cathedral, no date given.

Left: Tradition has it that this was the mitre of St Thomas à Becket. Made of Italian silk with English embroidery, it dates from between 1160 and 1220. Loaned by Westminster Abbey and displayed at the Victoria and Albert Museum. Illustration by the author.

During the medieval period, the area of the mitre on the left and the right of the *titulus*, which forms almost a triangular shape, also came to be decorated, often with geometrical medallions studded with jewels. Limoges Cathedral, nineteenth century.

St Nicholas is shown here wearing a magnificent mitre and superb cope with heavily embroidered orphreys. Part of an altarpiece commissioned by the abbot for his Abbey of Grimbergen and signed and dated (1563) by the little-known Jacques de Poindre. The Walters Art Museum.

to be used by bishops and archbishops, as well as the pope. There are many good extant examples in collections around the world, the most sumptuous being richly embroidered with gold and silver threads, galloons, semi-precious stones and pearls. Modern mitres are still made in the same way as they always have been, stiffened with canvas or similar fabric, and with decoration front and back and on the lappets or *infulae* – the two embroidered strips of fabric which hang from the back of a mitre and which are possibly the vestiges of the original sweat-band.

STOLE

According to many learned studies, the stole was derived from the *orarium*. As members of the clergy became subsumed into the Roman administration they were granted certain honours. The original intent of the *orarium* was to designate a person as belonging to a particular organization and to denote their rank within their group. In the fourth century it was worn as a vestment by deacons in the Eastern churches, and it was adopted somewhat later in the West. *Orarium* comes from the Latin term meaning 'to beg, plead, pray' but it was not until the twelfth century that the term 'stole' came into common usage. By the sixteenth century the stole had become the badge of bishops, priests and deacons.

Above:
A stole has one central cross at the back of the neck. This is the only required symbol; otherwise they are decorated in many different ways.

Far left:
At one time this purple velvet preaching stole with spade ends was very fashionable. It has cloth-of-gold inserts, rich gold bullion embroidery, and is edged with gold bullion braid and fringe.

Left:
A pale-coloured stole worn over a surplice for a wedding. The stole has appliqued designs of waves and fish, worked in the machine embroidery and hand painting which give a very distinctive style to Juliet Hemingray's designs.

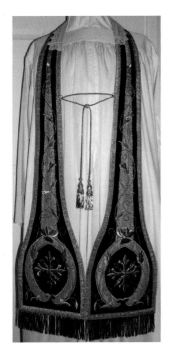

Right: A selection of Victorian stoles showing a wide range of hand embroidery techniques.

Below: Roman Catholic priests in lace cottas, and centre figure of cardinal in a biretta, c. 1910. The Roman Catholic church still uses far more lace on its cottas than other churches — usually in a deep band around the lower section.

Length and width vary from country to country and at times there have been some strange variations in the ends of the stole — a large spade version appearing in the late eighteenth century being a particularly ungainly, though popular variation which persisted well into the late nineteenth century in western Europe and is still seen today. Since the late twentieth century a small adaptation as to shape has occasionally been made to make the stole sit better across the shoulders.

In terms of decoration, only one cross is essential on a stole, at the back of the neck. No rules exist as to design or ornamentation, meaning that of all clerical dress stoles show the widest variation of decoration, colour and interpretation as far as design goes, and are frequently highly decorated with figures or pattern in gold and stones. Stoles today come in all colours and patterns, and designed for specific uses and occasions including baptism, marriage and death but also for industrial chaplains, chaplains to sea scouts etc.

SURPLICE OR COTTA

Both fuller and shorter than the alb, the surplice has full sleeves as opposed to the narrower sleeves of the alb. The surplice also hangs free and can be decorated with wide bands of lace along sleeve edges and the hem. The surplice, a convenient garment for liturgical purposes, permissible to all the clergy, was created by shortening and simplifying the alb (which became restricted to use at mass). The designation *superpelliceum* (from which the name surplice comes) comes from the old

William Laud was archbishop of Canterbury, 1633–45. His support for Charles I resulted in his beheading in the midst of the English Civil War. Here he is shown wearing a full-sleeved surplice caught at the wrists and a Canterbury cap. Published in 1779 by John Boydell, engraver.

Far left: A good illustration of a wide-sleeved surplice in an Ape cartoon, *Vanity Fair*, 1870.

Left: This Ape cartoon of the bishop of Oxford, Samuel Wilberforce (1805–73), shows the exaggerated sleeves of his surplice with the banded cuffs and a severe preaching gown. *Vanity Fair*, 1869.

Right: The modern preaching gowns and wide preaching scarves of the Church of Scotland.

Far right: Clergy have come in for a fair amount of ridicule in the past, as this print which accompanies a song of the time clearly shows. *The Vicar and Moses*, 1859.

custom, especially common in monastic circles, of wearing a linen garment over the fur coats necessitated by the long services in unheated and draughty religious buildings. The material is linen or now more commonly cotton. The cotta is simply a cut-down surplice.

THE PREACHING OR GENEVA GOWN

This is used mainly in the Reformed tradition and is derived from academic dress. It is sometimes worn with the academic hood or a scarf. Puritan dress following the Reformation consisted almost exclusively of the Geneva Gown, prayer bands and cassock, this austerity of dress reflecting their belief system – and continuing the idea that the Word of God is the important thing, and not a church full of expensive, luxurious and 'idolatrous' items, whether those be statuary or textiles. The Reformed and Evangelical churches of the west now still mainly adhere to this precept and continue the austerity of the visual, ministers sometimes wearing suits rather than gowns, and occasionally a tie rather than the clerical collar.

CIVILIAN DRESS

It is interesting to make a brief diversion into the area of civilian dress for the priest or vicar. Black with its sombre, serious image has long been used by the professions: academics, lawyers and clerks in holy orders. In fact since the late seventeenth century this mode of dress has changed very little. The early suit, a jacket with breeches which then became trousers, has long been the professionals' choice. The cassock was the recognised dress of the clergy but underwent changes as time went on, particularly for use outside church services. It was cut increasingly shorter until it barely reached the knees, and breeches were added to create what eventually emerged as the clerical coat familiar from the novels of Anthony Trollope and the cartoons of George Cruikshank and Spy. The dog collar, or clerical collar, as it should be called, was simply a development from the eighteenth-century white stock tied around the neck. By the 1880s the clerical collar had become a widely accepted part of a priest's everyday dress and, according to the Church of England's Enquiry Centre, the detachable clerical collar was invented by the Rev Dr Donald Mcleod, a Church of Scotland (Presbyterian) minister in Glasgow around this time. In the Reformed tradition ministers often wore preaching tabs, which projected from their clerical collar, and some still do. Anglican clergy generally wore the collar so that it was visible all the way round, but the Roman collar differed in that it was a black band of the cloth revealing the white collar centre front. This has become the regular uniform of those clergy, both Roman Catholic and Anglican, who wear the clerical shirt today.

The Most Reverend Edward White Benson, Archbishop of Canterbury, wearing the clerical coat which started life as a cassock. He also sports gaiters and a clerical aproned waistcoat fashionable at this time. Spy cartoon, *Vanity Fair*, 1887.

A Belgian priest on horseback during the first World War, wearing a stock and a traditional cleric's hat. Priests have always gone into battle, many doing valuable work as orderlies during the First World War.

FABRICS

'a cargo of gold, silver, jewels and pearls, fine linen, purple, silk and scarlet...' Revelation 18:12

VESTMENTS have been made and reused throughout the centuries. When examining old chasubles or altar frontals it is sometimes possible to see where cloth has been re-joined to form the new vestment or parament; or sometimes, as with the cushions and hangings at Hatfield House, home furnishings have been created from pillaged items. The fabrics used for vestments were expensive, and so were intended to last. With care, such fabric could be re-used many times before it was considered worn out. In 1890 over forty fragments of silk were retrieved from Archbishop Hubert Walter's tomb in Canterbury Cathedral (buried in 1205). Most of the fabric has been identified as late twelfth century and imported from Byzantium or Spain, some woven with patterns of birds and trees. Among the collection of items are slippers, buskins, amice apparel and stole, all of which are embroidered. The obvious conclusion is that these were indeed luxury goods. Not only were these expensive fabrics imported for fashionable costumes but they were also used to create vestments of the highest quality. Such items might perhaps be donated to a church or individual priest in memory of the departed or in thanks to God.

It is worth remembering that for centuries, services were conducted by candlelight, and so vestments were designed and made – using metallic fabrics, gold and metal threads, spangles and stones – to have a visual impact in this type of lighting. The increased importance that the reflected light lent to a vestment is an aspect mostly lost in an age of electricity. Worn or outdated vestments were often destroyed in order to extract the precious metals and stones embellishing them. In her essay *Stitches in Time*, Margaret Wade Labarge gives the example of Abbot Geoffrey of St Albans who gave to his monastery a chasuble that was covered with so much gold and precious stones that the succeeding abbot had it burnt to recover the gold. The value of items destroyed or redistributed is suggested in the records of materials

Opposite:
Detail of a brocatelle called Ludlow. A late nineteenth century Gothic design with central motif of a pineapple – this fabric was originally designed by F. J. Flanagan and is a mixture of cotton, viscose and metallic yarn.

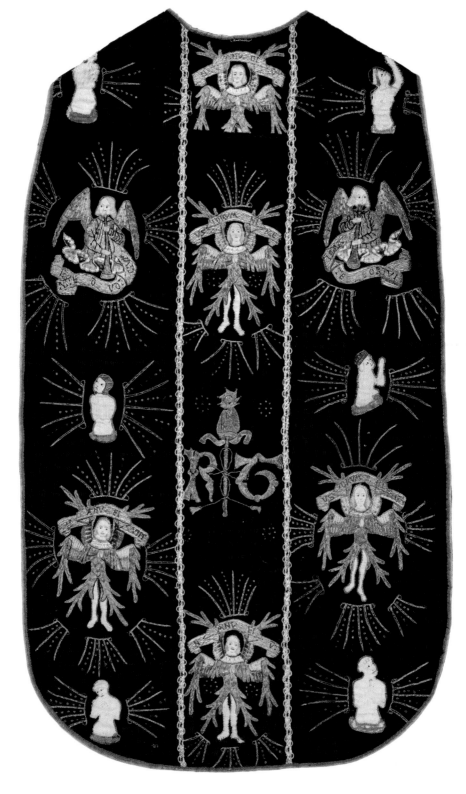

confiscated by Henry VIII's commissioners who, amongst many other items, removed 100 chasubles, 330 copes, 99 dalmatics, 288 albs, 103 maniples and eight mitres from Westminster Abbey in 1540.

The surviving vestments reflect the development of woven textiles. Before 1500 linen fabric was in general use until the late Middle Ages when cotton began to be imported into Western Europe. This came mainly from India, but from the sixteenth century also from the warmer areas of Asia and the Americas. Linen bases were used for embroidery before this time – the embroidery was worked before the pieces were applied, as with the apparels for the surplice. There are a few references to a fabric known as samite, which was a heavy fabric of silk, often woven with gold or silver threads, and used in the Middle Ages for clothing. George Tyack mentions that 'Richard of London gave an alb of red samite, embroidered in gold, in 1270'. Many of the fabrics used as a base for a cope or chasuble during the early medieval period came from the Middle East, imported through the main trading routes via Venice. But as the Arab weavers moved further west, eventually settling in Sicily and Southern Spain, new workshops were set up across Europe using their expertise.

From around the fifteenth century, silks, damasks and brocades (a rich fabric, usually silk, woven with a raised pattern, typically with gold or silver thread), woven in France and Italy, were widely used. Velvets were not known at all before the middle of the thirteenth century. They were invented by silk weavers in Italy and first mentioned in the west in 1277. Despite the use of these rich fabrics for copes, chasubles and stoles, they were also heavily embroidered with silk threads and metal wires.

Woven brocades, damasks and velvets – used in the first instance for grand dresses and gentlemen's coats – were exquisite silks of ornate pattern. As these fabrics were increasingly used in the making of vestments during the seventeenth and eighteenth centuries, there was a corresponding reduction in

Opposite:
This chasuble was recycled from a pall, a cloth used to cover a coffin, hence the dark colours. The embroidery dates from the early sixteenth century, but the shape is slightly later. Victoria and Albert Museum.

Detail of a nineteenth century chasuble of Gothic style made by the Belgian company Grossé. It shows a heavily worked and raised IHS symbol in gold threads embroidered on the back for an East facing celebration of the Eucharist.

Right: Detail of the fabric from an eighteenth-century chasuble. The design is a light-coloured floral fabric which would most probably have been used as a dress fabric. It has no obvious religious dimension but is typical of the fabrics used throughout the Baroque period.

Far right: A Victorian brocade with an all-over pattern of vines and wheat ears.

Opposite: A nineteenth-century jacquard woven orphrey using metal threads but applied to a late-eighteenth-century fabric which shows a fair amount of wear.

the use of embroidery. Pastel colours came to the fore and floral designs were much in evidence, not just in vestments but in fashionable clothing generally. The influence of the Baroque is apparent in the rich and flamboyant designs, the use of floral pattern and lighter colours and much gold in the form of galloons, braids and bullion fringing, all reflecting the fashions of the day but having very little to do with the ecclesiastical. The introduction of Joseph-Marie Jacquard's loom attachment in 1805 radically changed the designs available as well as the production methods, and the result was complex and very detailed woven scenes and patterns as well as more complex brocades and velvets. The Jacquard attachment used a series of pegs to lift individual shafts or sets of shafts to control the design more closely, giving a greater range of possibilities to the designer. As these more detailed designs became more available and easier to create, there arose a new form of mass production – orphreys could be woven incorporating Christian symbols, ready to be simply cut out and applied to the surface of the chasuble. With industrialisation came faster production in larger quantities and a standardisation of quality, meaning easier access to fabrics woven specifically for church use.

Many of the materials used for ecclesiastical embroidery have not changed for centuries, although modern embroiderers have the advantages of modern materials and methods of production. Silk and cotton can be made stronger with the addition of nylon, rayon or polyester without the result of a plastic 'hand' or feel to the cloth. Metallics, in the form of lurex, have become easier to include and do not tarnish. Fabrics can be made fire-retardant,

and mould and stain resistant. They can be woven in increasingly complex computer-designed patterns or in patterns resurrected from the past and given new life.

Braids, orphreys, cords and fringes were a separate but important industry and these items are still woven in the same way today as they have been for centuries. The embroiderers of the Middle Ages had a close link with goldsmiths, illuminators and wire drawers. The company of Toye, Kenning & Spencer, which was established

Selection of fabrics from a variety of European manufacturers, many woven from the patterns found in historical design books.

This shape of the Gothic chasuble shows the flowing lines achievable with an unlined fine white wool fabric; the modern machine-woven orphreys are a section of a jacquard woven fabric.

in 1655, still produces woven laces and narrow ribbons. In 1990 it incorporated Benton & Johnson (established in the seventeenth century) which makes gold wires and thread using traditional methods and machinery, enabling them to manufacture very small quantities. The gold wire is produced by coating copper wire in silver and then plating it with gold. Different thicknesses are produced by drawing it down to the required diameter by repeatedly stretching it very gently through a diamond die. This can then be turned into pearl purl – a wound wire looking like a tightly coiled spring, available as rough and smooth purl or bright check purl; bright check purl has a faceted, shiny surface, rough purl has a smooth, matte surface, smooth purl has a smooth, shiny surface, and check purl has a faceted, matte surface. The wire can also be converted into a flat form – called plate – using a plating mill in which the wire is drawn between two rollers up to thirty times, while gold thread is produced by spinning the wire around a cotton or silk core (this is often known as Passing or Japanese Gold).

Modern designers have access to a plethora of wonderful new materials as well as many of the traditional ones, and plastics, acrylic paint and nylon may be seen in use alongside silk and kid leather. Some modern work also seems to refer back to medieval raised embroidery using modern materials to pay tribute to these ancient techniques.

Some materials do not stand the test of time, as with this stole originally embroidered in silver threads. The orange core can be seen and the silver has tarnished to black.

COLOUR AND SYMBOLS IN VESTMENTS

'Of the blue, purple and crimson yarns they made finely worked vestments, for ministering in the holy place; they made the sacred vestments for Aaron; as the Lord had commanded Moses.' Exodus 39:1

FROM THE SOFT ELEMENTAL GREENS of Trinity to the powerful, vibrant reds of the Passion and through regal and despondent purple and violet to the spectacular, resplendent white and gold of Easter, colour has always been a most crucial element in church worship. Colour can create feelings of gladness, calm or joy, and this, combined with the symbols of Christianity, provides visual clues which are just as important for today's increasingly visually literate congregations as they have ever been. The medieval mason understood this use of the visual and of colour. Putting aside the colour of vestments, modern church interiors are sometimes seen as bland stage sets but our medieval brethren would have been presented with a spectacle of colour and light. Glimpses of this use of colour can sometimes be seen still in churches that escaped the damaging wave of the Reformation, and enthusiastic Victorian restorers. In some churches the damage is obvious, where faces of saints have been scratched out or obvious decoration removed. (One example of the type of work undertaken was the restoration of The Church of St Peter, Great Berkhamsted in 1870–1 by William Butterfield, whose other works included churches such as All Saints, Margaret Street in London. Butterfield's restoration involved the removal of some original features, including the obliteration of paintings on the pillars.) As Percy Dearmer pointed out in *The Parson's Handbook* in 1899, the use of differing colours was not set in stone until relatively recently. The Sarum Rite represented the general trend of liturgical colour use in northern Europe of the Middle Ages. In Britain, St Osmund, bishop of Salisbury in the eleventh century, brought about the uniformity of service known as the Sarum Rite, which was widely spread and used until the Reformation. Pope Innocent III (1198–1216) had also outlined a rule based on white for feasts, red for martyrs, black for penitential seasons and green at other times but many churches, especially the poorer parishes,

Opposite:
Hanging based on the Beatitudes using painted fabric, appliqué and machine embroidery. Work of the author.

39

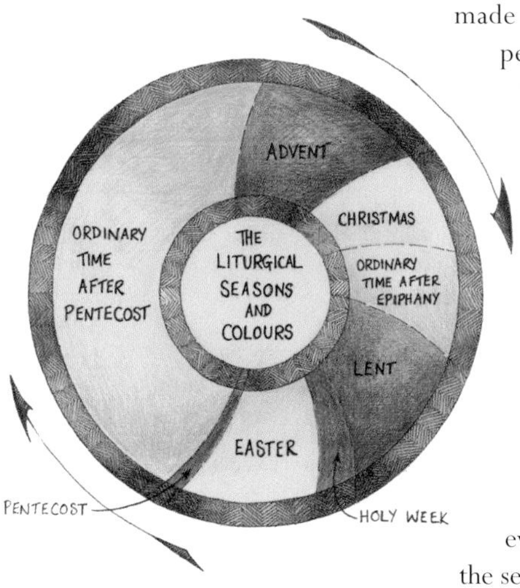
ADVENT
CHRISTMAS
ORDINARY TIME AFTER EPIPHANY
LENT
EASTER
ORDINARY TIME AFTER PENTECOST
THE LITURGICAL SEASONS AND COLOURS
PENTECOST
HOLY WEEK

Colours of the church year follow a set pattern as the seasons change through Advent, into Christmas and Epiphanytide, followed by Ordinary Time then into Lent and Easter and back through Ordinary Time, to the beginning of the Church year in Advent.

made do with a plain altar and a fair linen cloth and perhaps had no other covering. Other churches, perhaps with a wealthy local patron or family, may have had one or perhaps two altar cloths and maybe one decent chasuble for their priest. It was only the better endowed churches or cathedrals that possessed a variety of coloured vestments which were thought to be fitting for the church year. And in some cases the number of coloured vestments could be seen as a problem rather than a blessing. Percy Dearmer commented in 1932 on the vestments used: 'Indeed, so regularly were bright colours in use, that at York, in the year 1519, it was found advisable even in respect of funerals to specifically point out the seemliness of wearing black.'

The influence and availability of dyestuffs and new means of fabric production also influenced the colours used. For example, purple, due to its method of production, was for centuries only affordable for kings and emperors. The history of true purple dye is fascinating and its expense hints at why Christ's robe was always depicted in purple. Gold too, as a precious and rare material, only used for the robes of kings and the most important people, also had and still has its place in the production of the most elaborate vestments.

In the sixteenth century, the Reformed churches largely rejected coloured vestments used in worship – where Calvinist or Puritan, ministers were content with the black preaching gown worn over dark civilian clothes. As a counter to this however, the greatest elaboration in colour sequences was seen during the seventeenth and eighteenth centuries in the Roman Catholic Church.

With the nineteenth century and the renewed interest in the symbolism of colour the tradition of using a set colour sequence within the Roman Catholic, Anglican and Lutheran churches has been adopted and, with regional changes, also sees widespread use in the Reformed churches. Churches see the value of the changing seasons and festivals being represented on a symbolic level, using the language of colour to appeal to the emotions. With the adoption of a meaningful palette, and an increased understanding of its visual effects, colour is again being increasingly used in church environments to promote and enhance the space for worship.

On the whole, the use of colour during the Church year has settled into a roughly agreed pattern, with only subtle differences between the Anglican and Roman Catholic churches. It could be argued that these colour choices are pre-Christian, adopted by a faith for its own ends. The following is a very brief summary of the main colours used today; although there may be variations, these have been universally adopted.

Green is generally used during Trinity or Ordinary Time (the period of the liturgical calendar of the Christian church outside the feasts of Easter, Christmas, etc. The actual number of complete or partial weeks of Ordinary Time in any given year can total thirty-three or thirty-four, making it the longest period of use of one colour). It reflects nature and continuing life, the fecundity of nature, new growth.

White or gold is used for festivals as well as during the Christmas and Easter seasons. It symbolises the light given to the world, Christ in majesty and glory.

Purple is now used primarily for Advent and Lent. Both are times of reflection and contemplation. Advent is the period before Christmas, for reflection and repose before all the bustle of the holiday period, a time

For the festal season the choice is gold or white but usually a mixture of both. When it has the option of commissioning or purchasing a new set of vestments or paraments a church must consider the church interior into which these textiles are to be introduced. Design by Marie Brisou.

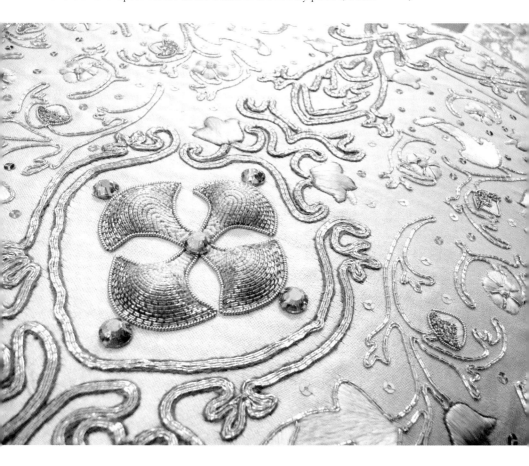

Though seen infrequently, red is a glorious colour reflecting the season of Pentecost. Orange-reds through to deep crimson and almost black-reds decorate this cope and mitre made with images of flames for the Right Reverend Dr Peter Selby. Judith Peacock 1991.

for peace and meditation and candles and prayer. Lent, occurring before Easter, has the same feel.

Red is used at Pentecost and for the martyrs. The symbolism is that of flames and blood.

Blue has long been a Marian colour in the west (a rich dark blue being the colour of emperors) – although further East it is mainly red that is associated with Mary – there are churches all over Europe dedicated to the Virgin Mary which display images of the Virgin dressed in blue. Some churches also possess rose-pink chasubles, in reference to Mary as the Mystical Rose, which are mainly used in the Roman Church for the third Sunday in Advent, and on Mothering (or Mid-Lent) Sunday.

Black was used much by the Victorians for funerals but soon superseded by purple. Lenten array, which in many places has fallen from favour, can occasionally be found in some churches or the altars may be left bare and the priest may simply use purple.

One cannot examine colour in church use without its symbolism. From a brief introduction into the uses of colour in ecclesiastical circles it is but a short step to looking at the symbols used in the western Church.

The use of the symbolic is at the heart of Christian worship, a separate but integral language. Dom Roulin pointed out in *Vestments and Vesture* that the number of symbols in fact used is very small, and always comes back to an original scriptural reference, despite the mania for emblems during the Middle Ages. It is the stoles, chasubles, copes and mitres which have all the decoration expended on them. Indeed the stole and chasuble in particular make wonderful canvases, onto which symbolism and colour can be 'painted', woven or embroidered. Very often the symbols also relate to the time of year within the Christian calendar or a particular aspect of a service, for example, the use of flames of the spirit at Passiontide or the use of wheat and grapes generally for the Eucharist.

Within Christian worship can be seen the use of water for baptism, the bread and wine at the Eucharist and the oil used for confirmation. These are dramatic, kinetic symbols and in fact many symbols – not only in the Christian faith but also in many others – are natural elements: water and fire; sun, moon and stars; living creatures and plants. A good example is that of the fish, a Christian symbol appearing either as a visual or literary image. The acrostic of the Greek for fish translates as, 'Jesus Christ, God's Son, Saviour', and it became a sign of recognition between the early persecuted Christians. The most familiar symbols representing the four evangelists are those of the eagle (St John), the ox (St Luke), the winged man (St Matthew) and the lion (St Mark), and many of

The sacrificial lamb references the sacrifice of Isaac in the Old Testament and the sacrifice of Christ in the New. A beautiful fragment of nineteenth-century French silk and silver thread brocade. This is one of the many machine-woven pieces specifically made to speed the creation of chasubles.

A variety of crosses and symbols, from left to right: top row, Christ the King, Chi Rho with Alpha and Omega, and Mary's Monogram; bottom row, Latin, Jerusalem and Tau crosses.

the saints are closely associated with particular symbols. Early representations of the twelve apostles are as a flock of sheep and there is the sacrificial lamb i.e. Christ. The most basic, and ubiquitous, symbol is the cross, a symbol of power and pain turning up in many forms whether Greek or Latin, the Tau or St Anthony's cross, the Jerusalem or Crusaders' cross. Lettering has been and is still widely used and there are specific letters, for example, IHS or IHC – the first three letters of Christ's name in Greek, all becoming part of the overall pattern. Alpha and Omega, in reference to 'I am the Alpha and Omega' or Chi Rho (CHRistos) are both still widely used.

The language of flowers should not be overlooked as it has been used in vestments since the Middle Ages when the symbolic meanings were of great importance and understood widely. The following are just a small selection of the floral symbols still in use: the lily represents the Virgin and appears in many paintings of the Annunciation; the pomegranate has been used in woven fabric design since the early medieval period and represents the hope of immortality and resurrection; the Glastonbury Thorn stands for the Nativity; the ten petals of the Passion Flower represent the twelve apostles, minus the one who denied Christ and the one who betrayed Christ; and, of course, wheat, grapes and the vine, representing the Eucharist.

By the end of the sixteenth century, vestments were beginning to lose their connection with a deeper symbolic meaning as the types of extravagant fabrics negated the use of extraneous embroidery or decoration. There was no scope at all for this extra dimension. However, with the Oxford Movement and others reinvigorating the interest in all things medieval, the interest in the symbolic was revived. The Oxford Movement began as a movement of High Church Anglicans which eventually developed into Anglo-Catholicism. The movement, whose members were often associated with the University of Oxford, argued for the reinstatement of lost Christian traditions of faith and their inclusion into Anglican liturgy and theology. The designers of the twentieth and twenty-first centuries have them to thank for this small start. It was not really until after the Second World War that there was a concerted intellectual questioning of the uses of symbols in church art, which resulted in fresh designs.

The Nuclear mitre was commissioned by Archbishop Mario Conti when Bishop of Aberdeen. The cross in amethyst and gold – which belonged to his mother – hovers over a volcanic or nuclear cataclysm, linking the creation of the world to the Nuclear age. The mitre is embroidered in collaged silks and Japanese gold and made by the Sacred Threads Guild, Glasgow.

EMBROIDERED DECORATION

'They also made the tunics, woven of fine linen … and the sash of fine twisted linen, and of blue and purple, and crimson yarns, embroidered with needlework.'
Exodus 39:27–29

IT IS FASCINATING that as humans we seem to have a need to embellish, decorate and generally enliven the surface of cloth which is not already a woven brocade or damask. Since the earliest times, clothes for use in worship, in many religions, have been embroidered to mark them out in richness and splendour. As the garments used specifically in the Christian tradition took their individual forms it was the early alb which first had embroidered decoration, executed in red thread in bands along the hem and cuffs. As the stole, chasuble and cope developed, their embellishment became increasingly ornate and the embroidery used more elaborate, the use of gold and plate threads, silks and precious stones often being incorporated.

Anglo-Saxon embroidery was highly regarded on the continent even before the advent of Opus Anglicanum, or English work, and was given as a valuable gift to foreign leaders. Thus, some of the earliest extant pieces of British church embroidery are in European collections. In Britain, the items in the treasury of Durham Cathedral are perhaps some of the best examples of this kind of work. The stole, maniple and girdle were thought to be an offering at the tomb of St Cuthbert in 934; it is recorded that King Athelstan visited the shrine of Cuthbert in Chester-le-Street at about this time and offered various gifts. Following on from this came the natural development of Opus Anglicanum. The Benedictine chronicler Matthew Paris of St Albans relates this story of Pope Innocent IV's admiration for Opus Anglicanum: 'about the same time (1245) my Lord Pope, having noticed that the ecclesiastical ornaments of certain English priests, such as choral copes and mitres, were embroidered in gold thread after a most desirable fashion, asked whence came this work? From England, they told him. Then exclaimed the pope, "England is for us surely a garden of delights, truly an inexhaustible well."'

Opposite:
Detail of a chasuble designed by Beryl Dean for All Saints Church, Newland. Although apparently an abstract design, on closer inspection one begins to see the myriad fish making up the pattern.

The most refined and exquisite examples of this elaborate and sought-after work were carried out in England between the 1130s and the 1340s. There are records of individuals who specialised in this sort of work – often men, but women were fine practitioners too. These individuals were highly regarded, some being paid well at a time of general poverty and serfdom. One of the primary ways in which Opus Anglicanum stands out from its European counterparts is the extreme quality and fineness but also the work and care which went into the planning and execution of designs. It took much skill, and still does, to work with gold threads. Any faces were worked in silks in split stitch, the direction in which stitches were worked giving life to the faces themselves. Much of the gold used was in the form of a laid or couched thread – the thread itself being a silk core wrapped with a finely beaten, extremely thin strip of gold. Another of the techniques used extensively is that of underside couching. Surface couching is simply the gold thread, laid onto the fabric surface (usually as a pair of threads) and stitched (couched) down with either a matching or contrasting thread but with a distinct pattern. The technique for which British embroiderers were famous, though, was that of underside couching, a more complex way of using a gold thread but one which gave a flexible gold surface. The gold threads were actually pulled through the fabric in a distinct, often diaper, pattern. On the continent the technique of *Or nué* was also used to great effect, particularly in Northern France and the Netherlands.

Much fine medieval work was destroyed during the Reformation, either stripped of its couched gold and semi-precious jewels or simply destroyed because of its use in 'idolatrous' worship. By the 1340s the standard of Opus Anglicanum was on the wane, and the destructive appearance of the Black Death from mainland Europe would finish off much of the embroidery industry. Whatever was produced after this time tended towards the derivative and poorly executed. During the fifteenth century 'new' materials began to be imported from France and Italy, the spectacular woven brocades and figured velvets. These fabrics did not require surface decoration in the same way as had been common for a couple of hundred years. They spoke for themselves, the richness and depth of colour and fine designs sufficient without further adornment.

Catherine de Medici of France was presented with a petition in 1586 on *The Extreme Dearness of Living*, which declaimed that: 'mills, lands, pastures, woods, and all the revenues are wasted on embroideries, insertions, trimmings, tassels, fringes, hangings, gimps, needlework, small chain stitching, quiltings, back stitching, etc: new diversities of which are invented daily'. The popularity of embroidery and the demand for rich and sumptuous garments became so great in Europe that there were various attempts to control what was seen as an excessive desire for finery. Edward III in 1363

Embroidered figure
from a chasuble
belonging to
Cardinal Newman
(see also page 14).
It shows a bishop
worked in silk
and gold threads
using a variety
of techniques.

decreed that: 'no one whose income was below four hundred marks per annum should wear cloth of gold or embroidery'.

One particular type of embroidery, appearing particularly in France at this time, was needlepoint. Scenes were worked onto even-weave canvas or linen in fine wools and could depict fairly complex scenes from the Old and New Testament, to be applied to a chasuble or altar frontal. Many fine extant examples appear in France and can frequently be found in small parish

An Italian mitre of 1500–50. The grotesque-style designs have been worked in silk embroidery threads, using a combination of long, short, satin and chain stitches. Victoria and Albert Museum.

church collections. In mainland Europe there are also examples of biblical scenes created in beadwork, which must have been especially heavy to wear.

The industrialisation that went on in Europe in the late eighteenth and nineteenth centuries meant that embroidery designs in their widest sense were available to far more amateur embroiderers. The publication of many ecclesiastical embroidery patterns now gave access to a far greater number of designs and design sources, and in this age of the haberdasher access to embroidery silks and fine materials was far more widespread. More women of the new leisured middle class were using their skills to create items for their local church, meaning that many of the vestments inherited by the

Embroidery from an eighteenth-century chasuble – silk and silver threads on a pale blue ground. Although degraded is easy to see the delicacy and quality in this vestment.

thousands of churches across Britain are from the mid- to late Victorian period. Many of these amateurs were accomplished embroiderers and their legacy is seen in many churches, where there can be many beautifully worked vestments but perhaps a loss of the full symbolic meaning which can appear in some of the best work of the time.

Another influential change in the creation of vestments has been the increased use of the sewing machine for embroidery. The early Cornely or chain-stitch machine is still in use. The first successful machine was developed by French engineer Antoine Bonnaz in 1865. Ercole Cornely developed the machine further, to produce both chain and moss stitches, at his factory in Paris. Free machine embroidery is employed by many designers and more powerful and complex machines are now widely available to those interested in making vestments for the church. Machine-embroidery threads have developed to include a vast range – metallic, neon, invisible and vanishing. Options for design and production have expanded with the development of new technologies such as computer-controlled multi-head embroidery machines, laser-cutting technology and transfer and laser printing. The possibilities may seem endless but designers still face the same constraints and choices, trying to ensure that the technique does not dominate the use and meaning of the piece.

Despite the widespread use of machine embroidery, goldwork is still one of the favourite techniques for embroiderers commissioned to make church vestments. This embroidery is worked by hand onto fabric stretched on a frame and uses a variety of specific materials: pearl purl, with its coil-like appearance, is first gently stretched to open up the coils, and then can either be cut into short lengths and applied as a bead or, more usually, couched onto the surface fabric in one length. Rough and smooth purl or bright-check

Following spread: An Italian design from the late eighteenth century, showing the embroidery to be carried out on a fiddleback chasuble. The heavy swags and elaborate floral patterns, very similar to the previous image, are typical of this period.

A detail of an early-twentieth-century chasuble from Batcombe Church, Somerset. A Cornely machine, producing chain stitch, was used for this striking design.

A page from *The Architect*, 1879, shows the design for an embroidered mitre by William Burges, architect and designer of Cardiff Castle and Castell Coch. It also shows a detail of the stitches used for the embroidery.

purls are soft, wormlike coils cut into short lengths and used as a bead. Plate, as its name suggests, is a narrow, flat metal strip which can be couched into place. Passing is the most basic and common thread used in goldwork; it consists of a thin strip of metal wound around a core of cotton or silk. For gold thread this core is typically yellow, or in older examples orange; for silver, the core is white or grey. It comes in a variety of thicknesses and is couched

down with contrasting coloured threads. It is generally couched as a double strand and the ends pulled through to the back of the work and tied off. It is also used for *Or nué* and underside couching. The latter was used throughout the Middle Ages, but is not widely used now as it is a difficult technique to master. Some embroidered motifs appearing on chasubles and copes in particular are three-dimensional in execution and use a particular technique known as raised or stump work. This utilises padding, whether wooden blocks or tightly packed wool or felt, to raise the surface to be embroidered.

Close-up of an elaborate nineteenth-century purple velvet maniple with highly raised metal embroidery and heavy bullion fringing.

A selection of Goldwork materials including purls, plate, spangles (gold metal sequins) and passing threads.

THE MAKERS

'He has filled them with skill to do every kind of work done by an artisan or by a designer or by an embroiderer in blue, purple, and crimson yarns.' Exodus 35:35

ON 25 October 1561, Queen Elizabeth I granted The Worshipful Company of Broderers – or The Brotherhood of The Holy Ghost of the City of London – its first charter. The company had been formed many years earlier to promote and protect the craft of embroidery, and as one of the many guilds, was important to the standing of that craft. There is a connection between embroiderers and illuminators of the medieval period, in that the art was interchangeable. Those who could draw or produce beautiful designs were often commissioned to draw or paint designs onto cloth to be embroidered. In an essay by Barbara Gordon entitled *Whips and Angels*, she explores the connection, as well as the lesser-known craft of cloth painting, of which very little survives. She refers to the Mitre d'Eveque, which was painted in grisaille on silk samite around 1360 using the same imagery on any embroidered mitre of the same period, but would most probably have cost far less. Between 1239 and 1244, a Mabel of Bury St Edmunds regularly appears in the accounts from the royal records of Henry III, being commissioned to embroider items for the king's use. In November 1239 she was commissioned to make a chasuble and offertory veil for the king's use and allowed £101 for her expenses. The vestments were completed in late summer 1241, and lined with cloth of gold after being approved by other embroiderers, which seems to have been normal practice at this time. Mabel is cited by many historians but she is one of many who would have been employed at this time. Much of the work for which they were commissioned was admittedly for church use, but a proportion was also secular and much beautiful work also done 'in house' by ladies of leisure. Mary, Queen of Scots, who embroidered away the hours of her long imprisonment, employed Pierre Oudry between 1560 and 1567 and later Charles Plouvart as her embroiderers. Some embroiderers managed to make a very good living from supplying the great and the good. Some of the

Opposite:
Heavy silver lace attached to a purple silk chasuble – not the original ground.

57

Advertisement for Watts & Co. noting 'All articles from designs of George Frederick Bodley, George Gilbert Scott and Thomas Garner'. From the *Illustrated Guide to the Church Congress, 1897*.

foremost would be involved not just with the supply of embroidered goods however, but also fine imported fabrics and the gold threads used for the work. In the Records of Embroiderers' Almshouses, 1587–1890, David Smith, an embroiderer of London, bequeathed money to Christ's Hospital for the building of six almshouses for six poor widows. After the almshouses were sold in 1863–5, it appears that the widows continued to receive financial support.

There has been a long tradition of convent involvement in the production of embroidery for vestments and although this almost entirely disappeared for several centuries in Britain, by 1870 there were 220 Roman Catholic women's communities. The importance of the embroidery workrooms to their income was vital and they contributed immensely to the increase of well-made vestments. Since the start of the twentieth century there has been a gradual decline in the number of convents, however some communities are still active in their embroidery and production of vestments.

At the beginning of the nineteenth century, several things coincided to encourage a renewed interest in embroidered vestments. In Britain especially, the re-establishment of Roman Catholicism, the beginnings of the Oxford Movement and the Ecclesiological Society (which started life as the Cambridge Camden Society in 1839) all looked for the restoration of dignity and beauty in worship. Pauline Johnstone's book *High Fashion in the Church* gives an excellent account of the holistic approach taken by many designers of this period.

The 1830s saw the establishment of some companies which are still upholding the tradition of fine ecclesiastical embroidery and vestment production. In her book *English Church Embroidery 1833–1953*, Mary Schoeser gives a full account of the development of church textiles through this period of growth. Companies which came to the forefront in Britain were those such as Watts & Co, established in 1874 by three of the nineteenth century's most important architects – George Frederick Bodley, Thomas Garner and George Gilbert Scott junior – and who worked with several British convent communities. They expounded the importance of good craftsmanship and excellence in design. The company J. Whippell & Co. was based in Exeter. The family came from the West Country and can be traced back to the sixteenth century, but set up a specialist grocer in 1802 which gradually expanded into the church furnishing company it is today. Vanpoulles, based in Crawley, West Sussex, has been in existence since 1908 and continues to produce exquisite pieces in its workrooms; it has close links with textile design company Slabbink in Bruges which weaves modern, lightweight fabrics.

By the late nineteenth century a more formal embroidery training had become available. In 1872 the School of Art Needlework (later to become the Royal School of Needlework) was founded by Lady Victoria Welby, firstly to revive a craft which had fallen into disuse and secondly to provide training for employment for educated women who would otherwise find themselves living in poverty. Then in 1906, sixteen former students of the Royal School of Needlework founded The Embroiderers Guild to represent the interests of embroidery, to undertake or support research, and to educate the public in the history and art of embroidery. Across Europe at this time, art schools and training institutions were also playing a significant part in improving design standards.

However, one designer appearing in the 1950s was to change things in Britain. Beryl Dean, a teacher and embroiderer, wrote a book which

A mitre for the Episcopal Bishop of Glasgow and Galloway by Georgina Oliphant in 1904, showing the Arts and Crafts movement's love of the gothic. It was possibly made for the consecration of Archibald Ean Campbell at St Mary's Church, Glasgow, on 24 February 1904.

Mitre for the bishop of London, Richard Chartres, commissioned by The Worshipful Company of Weavers. Designed and made by Rozanne Hawksley, 1998, using symbols and imagery reflecting the interests and strengths of the bishop as well as church tradition.

Five members of
the clergy wearing
orphreys. From
left to right,
Canon Hugh Boyle,
wearing St Enoch,
Mother of Mungo;
Bishop Conti of
Aberdeen (later
Archbishop of
Glasgow) wearing
St Margaret;
Cardinal Winning
wearing St Mungo:
Bishop Renfrew
of Motherwell
wearing
St Columba;
the Abbot of Fort
Augustus wearing
St Ninian. All wool
embroidery on
canvas by the
Sacred Threads
Guild.

spurred many designers to discover a new and exciting scope for design within ecclesiastical embroidery. Beryl Dean's designs opened up a whole new world of the possible to professional and amateur alike with her book *Ecclesiastical Embroidery*, published in 1958. It included a historical survey of ecclesiastical embroidery, an explanation of symbolism, and technical details. She encouraged the use of new and modern materials alongside the old and traditional and experimented with textures, form and symbolism. She influenced a number of leading designers of church embroidery in Britain including Cath Whyte, Jane Lemon and Maurice Strike, Hannah Frew Paterson and more recently Juliet Hemingray, Alice Kettle, and Rozanne Hawksley. Many designers gather together small groups of talented enthusiasts and professionals who have taken

A modern mitre
using machine
embroidery in
metal threads, and
traditional gold
hand embroidery
with garnets and
pearls. Sarah Bailey,
2009.

up the challenge of producing modern church textiles, for example the Sacred Threads Guild in Glasgow, or the Sarum Group in Salisbury. These designers have themselves inspired many others to create new, exciting work for the church in Britain and beyond.

The options for a church seeking new vestments are now many and varied, with long-standing companies such as Vanpoulles, Watts, F. A. Dumont and others providing good-quality and value-for-money off-the-peg garments. There are also companies that deal exclusively in the second-hand and antique market, though many churches see more sense in purchasing new. The internet has also opened up the market in vestments made and embroidered in South America, the Russian Federation and India, and many North American and western European companies are finding new markets amongst the emerging Christian communities of the Far East. But there continues to be a steady market for the private commissioning of vestments made to the exact requirements of priest or church.

From the middle of the twentieth century there has been a flowering of interest in designing vestments for the church, particularly in Britain. Modern vestment designers are not always embroiderers or dressmakers, but may instead be fashion designers, sculptors or weavers. There has been an increasing number of artists and designers working in Europe and North America who are creating thoughtful, well-produced vestments with an appreciation for the symbolic aspects of their work.

This book has only scratched the surface of this subject; the few vestments shown represent thousands of hours, paid and unpaid, spent on their creation and the work which continues to fill churches with colour and pageant. The Christian church always changes slowly and church vestments are part of its continuing life in the west. Textiles, and vestments in particular, may not be indispensable to the Gospel but they are still important as part of the church's visual language, the theatre of worship. Whether the plain black cassock or preaching gown or the elaborately embroidered cope and mitre of a bishop, they tell the story of the church and link everyone who sees them to its continuing history and tradition.

The Maolrubha Detached Orphrey (c. 2001). The orphrey was a gift from Netta Ewing and the Sacred Threads group to Father Jamie MacNeill, who was appointed priest to the Isle of Skye, an historic appointment, being the first since the Reformation. The design shows a fairly bleak Hebridean sky and landscape at the top, with fragments of a stone cross and memories of the Book of Kells and its 'carpet pages' farther down. It symbolises the warm richness of the Celtic faith in a cold wilderness climate.

BIBLIOGRAPHY

Baumgarten, Barbara Dee. *Vestments for all Seasons*. Morehouse Publishing, 2002.

Cole, Alan. *Ornament in European Silks*. Debenham and Freebody, 1899. (available to read online through Google books)

Dawson, Barbara. *Metal Thread Embroidery*. B. T. Batsford Ltd, 1968.

Dean, Beryl. *Ecclesiastical Embroidery*. B. T. Batsford Ltd, 1958.

Dean, Beryl. *Church Needlework*. B. T. Batsford Ltd, 1961.

Dean, Beryl. *Embroidery in Religion and Cermonial*. B. T. Batsford Ltd, 1981.

Dearmer, Percy. *The Parson's Handbook*. OUP, 1932.

Ferguson, George. *Signs and Symbols in Christian Art*. OUP, 1954.

Hands, Hinda M. *Church Needlework*. The Faith Press, 1920.

Ireland, Marion P. *Textile Art in the Church*. Abingdon Press, 1966.

Johnstone, Pauline. *Byzantine Tradition in Church Embroidery*. Argonaut Inc., 1967.

Johnstone, Pauline. *High Fashion in the Church*. Maney Publishing, 2002.

Kendrick, A. F. *English Needlework*. A & C Black, 1967.

Lemon, Jane. *Metal Thread Embroidery*. B. T. Batsford Ltd, 1987.

Norris, Herbert. *Church Vestments: Their origin and development*. Dover 2002. (Originally published by E. P. Dutton 1950)

Pocknee, C. E. *Liturgical Vesture*. A. R. Mowbray & Co., 1959.

Roulin, Dom. E. O. S. B. *Vestments and Vesture*. Sands & Co, 1931.

Schoeser, Mary. *English Church Embroidery 1833–1953*. Watts & Co. Ltd, 1998.

Staniland, Kay. *Medieval craftsmen: Embroiderers*. British Museum Press, 1991.

Tyack, Reverend George. *Historic Dress of the Clergy*. William Andrews & Co., 1897.

Whyte, Kathleen. *Design in Embroidery*. B. T. Batsford Ltd, 1969.

Catholic Women's Devotional Bible, NRSV, The Zondervan Corporation, 2000.

Plus a variety of learned papers published on the web:

Gordon, Barbara. 'Whips and Angels – Painting on Cloth in the Medieval Period' 2001.

Peacock, Judith 'The Poor Relation – Ecclesiastical Embroidery', *Embroidery* Magazine, Embroiderers guild, 2008.

Townsend, Gertrude. 'Notes on Embroidery in England during the Tudor and Stuart Periods' 1961.

Wade Labarge Margaret. 'Stitches in Time: Medieval Embroidery in its Social Setting' 1999.

PLACES TO VISIT

Any of the great cathedrals in Europe during a festival service will have a magnificent collection of vestments on show, worn by the clergy. Frequently vestments are not items regularly on show to the public unless they have some special reason for being so, as with the Beryl Dean chasuble at All Saints Church or the Cardinal Newman vestments at Abbotsford House. Many museums may have the odd one or two vestments or, as with the Victorian and Albert, have a good collection of important and early pieces on constant show.

Victoria and Albert Museum, Cromwell Road, London SW7 2RL.
   Telephone: 020 7942 2000. Website: www.vam.ac.uk
St Mungo Museum of Religious Life and Art, 2 Castle Street, Glasgow G4 0RH.
   Telephone: 0141 276 1625. Website:
   www.glasgowlife.org.uk/museums/our-museums/st-mungo-museum
The Burrell Collection, Pollok Country Park, 2060 Pollokshaws Road,
   Glasgow G43 1AT. Telephone 0141 287 2550. Website:
   www.glasgowlife.org.uk/museums/our-museums/burrell-collection
All Saints Church, Newland, Forest of Dean.

Hubert's dalmatic was saucily split
to mid-thigh

INDEX